Passive Income

Complete Guide on How to Make Money and Create Financial Freedom

Andrew D. Hoskins

Your Gift!

We want to show our appreciation that you support our work, so we have put together a gift for you.

Just visit the link on the last page of this book to download it now.

We know you will love this gift.

Thanks!

Table of Content

SUMMARY — 5

INTRODUCTION — 5

CHAPTER 1 – SELL AN EBOOK — 7

Points For Making a Book — 8

Marketing Your Book — 9

Exercise — 9

CHAPTER 2 – CREATE A BLOG — 10

How Do You Earn Money? — 11

Tips For Your Blog — 12

Exercise — 13

CHAPTER 3 – CREATE A REVIEW SITE — 14

Points For Creating a Review Site — 15

Avoiding Bias — 16

Exercise — 17

CHAPTER 4 – CREATE AN APP — 18

Points For Creating An App — 18

Derivative Apps Are Useful — 19

Can An Outside Party Help? — 20

Exercise	21

CHAPTER 5 – PRODUCT DESIGN — 22

What Products Can You Sell?	23
Tips For Designs	23
Exercise	24

CHAPTER 6 – CREATE YOUTUBE VIDEOS — 24

What Are Your Videos About?	26
How Many Videos?	27
Can You Choose Your Sponsor?	27
Exercise	28

CHAPTER 7 – RENTING OUT ITEMS — 30

A Word of Caution	32
Exercise	33

CHAPTER 8 – RENTAL PROPERTY INVESTING — 35

FACTORS TO CONSIDER BEFORE INVESTING	38
SEARCHING FOR RENTAL PROPERTY	41
BUILD A TEAM OF EXPERTS	43
SELF-EDUCATION	45
CASH FLOW CALCULATIONS	47

MAINTAIN YOUR RENTAL PROPERTY	50
LOAN APPLICATION	52

CONCLUSION 56

Summary

The exciting world of passive income is the focus of this valuable book. Read on to learn about how passive income works.

This is a form of income that entails very little effort on your part over time. It requires a bit of an investment and some actual effort at the start but after a while it becomes all the more beneficial. This effort at the start typically involves creating a base for earning money.

The money you earn comes from sales of products or services you offer, advertising revenues, referral points and much more. The ways how you can earn money through passive income are indeed varied.

This guide will give you information on how to make money through passive income. Exercises are included in each chapter to help you see what you can do to get money and make any kind of passive income plan work to your benefit.

Introduction

You can make money online in a variety of ways but some of the best options involve ones that you don't have to put in much of an effort for. The exciting world of passive income is something you need to explore as it provides you with a great way to make money without doing much in the process.

Passive income is one of the more intriguing points of making money that you could ever consider. This refers to income that you earn from some investment or other work endeavor in which you are not actively involved in.

Here's an example of how passive income works in general. Let's say that you have some property, website or another item that you own or operate. You might have other people use it or access it in some other way.

But the key is that you would not have anything to do with the regular operations or management of the assets that you hold. Rather, you are letting out your investment to others.

Over time you will eventually make money off of that investment or other opportunity. The best part is that you will not have done all that much to keep it running. That is, you are earning money in the background.

Of course, this is just one of the ways how you could earn passive income. Several options are listed in this guide.

The potential for you to earn money through passive income is significant. There are no limits as to what you can earn. But to get the most money, you have to know what to do and how to do it the right way.

This guide will help you recognize the many ways how you can earn passive income. These include many solutions that are simple and easy to follow.

Each chapter ends with an exercise to help you figure out how you can complete a specific task. This is to help you fully understand how to get a quality passive income project to work.

The options for passive income are vast and worthwhile. Let's take a look at what you can do.

Chapter 1 – Sell an Ebook

People are always interested in reading. If anything, today's digital devices have only made it easier for people to read, what with them being able to load up electronic books. Selling a book is always a smart idea to consider.

It is very easy to sell ebooks online. Places like Amazon have become especially popular for how they allow people to list their own books online and sell them.

With such a setup, you will make money by getting a cut of the sales from each book you have. The place that hosts your book sale will end up getting a part of the sales as it is responsible for putting your book out there.

There is a good potential for you to make a great deal of money after you write a book and post it online. Best of all, you don't necessarily have to make something far too long. A book that is only around 50 to 80 pages – or even something as long as this book – will be good enough. The key is to write something that is appealing to people in some way.

Points For Making a Book

As you write a book, you have to think about how you will make it stand out and visible. To start, think about the subject that your book will cover. Look at what you might be interested in writing about and what you feel is appealing to audiences. Don't just write about anything; write about something that you know is worthwhile and is of interest to you. Be invested in your work.

Also, you should look at the kind of book you will write. While it is true that fictional works can be entertaining, books about certain real life topics or tutorials on how to do special things are appealing.

For instance, if you enjoy gardening then maybe you could use your knowledge of that field and put it into a book. It would be even better if you have a very specific field of work or interest to write about. This could include points relating to how to grow certain types of vegetables or how to maintain a garden during the winter season.

You also have to ensure the book is detailed and long enough. Don't try and make your ebook as long as a massive paperback novel. You don't need to make something that long just to earn passive income.

Marketing Your Book

After you are done writing your book, market it on social media, blog sites and other spots of value. The key is to market your work at places where people who might be interested in your book would see your messages at.

Going back to the gardening example, you would be better off marketing that book on blogs dedicated to the subject.

Be willing to answer questions that people might pose to you when you are promoting your book. Show them that you can answer questions that come about at any time.

Exercise

To prepare your book, think about what you are interested in writing on. After that, see if you can narrow down that interest to a very specific niche.

Look at the points you might want to highlight in your book. Prepare a good outline for that book as you start to write it. Make sure it is concise and sensible without going overboard. Check on how well the book looks after you are finished writing it. Don't publish something that might appear unprofessional or poorly edited.

After writing your book, make sure it is loaded up onto the proper websites that sell ebooks. Amazon is obviously a good choice but look around elsewhere too. Be sure to also promote your work on blogs, social media sites and so forth to drum up interest.

Create multiple books if possible. Make them about the same niche or interest. Show that you've got a vested desire for something and that you want to share it with anyone who is interested.

Chapter 2 – Create a Blog

Are you interested in talking about all sorts of stuff? Maybe creating a blog is a great idea.

Blogging is appealing for how it provides people with a way to tell others about all sorts of things that they are interested in.

A blog is great in that you can write about anything and update it as often as you want.

Do you want to create a blog relating to your favorite sports team?

Maybe there's a music or movie genre you are interested in and you want to write about the newest
developments in that field or about its history. There are no limits as to what you could talk about.

As you develop your blog, you will express yourself as an authority figure on something of value. Sharing your knowledge consistently and thoughtfully is important to do. This helps you show that you definitely understand whatever it is you want to highlight in your work.

How Do You Earn Money?

You will earn more off of your blog through affiliate marketing. This is a process where you post a series of advertisements onto your site. These ads link to places that sell various items.

When a visitor clicks on an ad or link from your site, that person goes to a page through your referral link. That person orders a product or service within a certain timeframe. You then receive a substantial cut of the sale because you were the one that recommended a person to that site.

This is great provided that you have affiliate links that are relevant to whatever your blog is about. When you write about something relating to those links, it becomes easier for you to encourage people to visit those sites you are trying to steer them towards.

This comes as you are showing yourself as an authority on whatever you are blogging about. Write regularly about something you know and show your interest. Express to people that what you want to say is worthwhile and that there are plenty of intriguing things to explore with regards to something of importance to you.

Tips For Your Blog

When writing your blog, write about something that you are definitely interested in. Don't just write about something popular that you might not be all that invested in.

Keep your blog updated regularly. Establish a sensible schedule where a certain number of updates will be produced in a given time. You could update your blog on specific days of the week or every two or three days, for instance. Keep that schedule consistent so people will know when to expect new stuff off of your site.

Allow people to share things on your blog. Offer plenty of social media connections on your site.

Create links between your site and other places that cover similar interests. The odds are there are plenty of people out there who are running their own websites who want to share their likes and values.

Most importantly, avoid making your site look like a deliberate attempt at making money. Any links that you put into your site should be incorporate naturally without sounding like you're writing blatant advertisements.

Exercise

To establish a blog, find a proper hosting site. There are various free sites that will help you to host a blog.

You also have the option to create your blog through a website creator. Various programs such as this offer plug-ins and interface setups to help you create a visually stunning site. The cost associated with using such a creator will vary though. Watch for the costs involved with getting a domain name for the blog set up too.

Figure out a few posts that you want to produce. After that, create a schedule for when you are going to get those posts out. Make sure the schedule is consistent and regular.

Chapter 3 – Create a Review Site

Shopping has changed in the past few years. Today people go online to find information on things they want to order. Customers want to get details on as many items as possible. It is all about finding products that they know are worthwhile and are easy to enjoy.

There are many websites out there that let you compare different types of products or services. You might see a site that compares numerous computer antivirus programs. You could also see a place that reviews airline reward and loyalty plans.

Creating your review or comparison site is great for passive income. Such a site gives you the opportunity to use various affiliate programs to earn money. You will also provide visitors with a sensible service where people can understand everything in a certain category.

When you establish a review site, you will post links to sites where people can buy those products or services from. Make sure you sign up for their affiliate programs so you are properly rewarded though.

Points For Creating a Review Site

As you establish your review site, you will have to watch for how well the page is organized. You will have to post several products of a certain type on your site.

Your page will only work if you actually understand whatever it is you are trying to discuss. Reliable review sites are always written by people with a vested interest in in the things they want to talk about. Share information on what you know and give readers the opportunity to purchase items.

Consider the type of product or service you plan on reviewing. Choose an option that you know you are invested in or is something you understand.

Check up on different products that are available in that category. You don't necessarily have to buy them; you just need to look and see what these feature and how they might be different from one another. Create a series of categories that you will review and compare items based on.

Aim to get as many products as possible. Always use the newest products that are available in your reviews.

Update the site as often as needed when new things come out on the market. Letting people know about the latest items in a certain field is important as it gives you the opportunity to inform people about something of value.

Don't forget to add updates on any existing things that you have already discussed on your site.

Don't forget to include plenty of visual bits of information around your site. Pictures or screenshots of something are useful provided that you can get the copyrights or clearances to use them. Charts and other helpful visual aids especially make it easier for people to compare items and see what makes them different from each other.

Avoiding Bias

Biases are concerning problems that might come about when you're trying to create a review site. People might assume that you are biased towards one particular product or service. The concern is especially clear if you like one particular option that you are reviewing over all others.

You must ensure that you look at all items you review on your own. Avoid taking in money or other free offers from outside parties. The offers would often try and influence your opinion and might provide you with information that is heavily skewed in its favor.

Read the language you use on your website as well. Using extreme adjectives or overly positive or negative language can be a dangerous concern.

Be certain when writing that you check on everything you prepare. Think about whether some of the things you are writing are outlandish or if they are sensible.

Also, cover both the pros and cons of whatever you are writing about. Do not skew heavily towards one or two concepts or else it might be difficult for you to write something.

Exercise

To create a review or comparison site, start by looking at a certain topic or niche you have a strong interest in. Maybe you know of some field that you have used several products or services in.

Create a series of categories and other factors that you will compare and review individual products by. Use a series of subjects that are relevant to the matter.

Prepare an affiliate program with a particular place that sells certain items. Amazon has the most commonly used affiliate program that you can work with for your review site although you are free to look around to see what else is available for your use.

Chapter 4 – Create an App

Have you taken a look at the Google Play Store or the Apple App Store lately? You might notice that there are loads of different apps out there.

These include apps for everything. You can find some that focus on budgeting your money or organizing lists. You could also find some gaming apps that focus on a vast variety of activities.

Did you know that you can create an app to get passive income? This is possible as you will get a significant amount of money for every time that someone purchases and downloads your app.

Points For Creating An App

To earn passive income when creating an app, you have to think about a good program that you wish to create. You have to option to create any kind of app that you want but you should still think about how well such a program is to be run. The functionality of the program is critical to its success. Create a program that you know has a potential audience. Make the app run to where it will not be too hard to use.

As you create your app, look at how that program will be organized. Create an outline for that program based on what you want to incorporate into the setup.

The app must be distinct and appealing. More importantly, the program should also stand out in some manner. With so many apps out there, it is easy for yours to be lost in the pile of other programs for download. Create apps that you know will be visible and stand out in a special manner.

Derivative Apps Are Useful

One option to look into when creating an app is to think about a derivative app. This is a type of program which is similar to another app but has been redesigned or targeted to fit the needs of another party.

For instance, an app that helps with designing landscapes for the outside of a home could be reprogrammed to focus on how to design a den or basement or other large room inside a home. Anything could work if you think carefully about how you are targeting a specific group.

Can An Outside Party Help?

There are times when you might need some extra help for getting a mobile app ready. Maybe your ideas are a little more complex or you have very little technical knowledge for how to set up a program. But the cost of such services might be too high depending on how intense the support you need might be.

You could always contact freelance help or an app creator business to help you with setting up a quality app. Such services will analyze your needs and prepare a technically functional program that is right for you.

Many app production teams manage coding functions to create apps that run properly. More importantly, they are apps that work on a variety of mobile devices.

Outside parties can also assist you in getting such apps loaded onto proper marketplaces. A full listing that includes keywords, descriptions and screenshots of your app will be created by someone and submitted to the Google Play and Apple App Stores.

Such an outside service works if you have a great idea and you know everything you want to incorporate in your work. But to make this run right, you must look at the cost associated with the service. Compare the cost versus the potential profits you would get off of the app.

Depending on the estimated cost, it might be best for you to just learn how to create a good app through a certain program.

Exercise

To start, find a program that allows you to create an app. There are various software programs to choose from including Appery.io, Mobile Roadie, TheAppBuilder, Appy Pie and AppMachine. All of these programs give you a variety of options for preparing your own apps although the cost for getting one of these to work will vary.

After that, read on about how the program works. As you do this, consider the type of app you will prepare. Look at the goals you want to get out of it and how you would envision people making that app.

Establish an outline for the app and then prepare it based on what you feel is appropriate for its use. Check on how well the program is to be run so you will have a clear idea of how it might work.

Chapter 5 – Product Design

Today you could design a variety of products if you have the skills. You might be an artist who has many designs for shirts, for instance. You could also design websites with particular templates or schemes that can be appropriated by other people.

Product design jobs are appealing passive income options. This is a great process that works with a few important steps. To start, come up with a design template for something of value. Think about how a template for a website could be utilized, for instance. Look at how the site might be arranged or how individual bars, columns and other features are organized.

After you come up with a design you must go and sell that to someone who will offer products or services that incorporate the design. For the website design template, send it off to a site that sells such options for those who wish to create their own pages.

As the product is available, you will get a profit off of sales relating to that design. Every time someone buys what you have, you will earn a cut of the profits. This adds up over time and gives you a huge payout after a while.

What Products Can You Sell?

The things that you could sell are especially worthwhile. Design templates can be easily prepared and offered to websites that cater to people aiming to create their own pages. Meanwhile, art designs for shirts, laptop covers, cell phone cases and stickers could be sent to many crafts sites. These places take your design patterns and print them onto a variety of items. The designs are typically printed on demand as sometimes such designs might not be big enough to where they could be mass-produced.

Over time, you will get loads of money when you have plenty of designs available. Creating unique and distinctive designs does more than show off your intriguing style. It also gives people different options for showing off their interests. The fashionable designs of what you have to offer will make a real difference.

Tips For Designs

Look at your creativity skills. Are you are great cartoon artist? Maybe you are good with promotional art. Whatever the case, focus your designs based on things you have a strong vested interest in.

After this, look for a niche of value to you. It might be interesting to create artistic designs that focus on a variety of specifics that are interesting. You might be impressed at how different topics can be represented by unique designs.

Exercise

Think about an artistic design that might be appealing. Choose a design plan that reflects what you like and what you enjoy doing. Be creative when coming across something that stands out and offers a distinct look into your psyche.

Create a few drafts of a design before submitting it to a website. Look at the design and think about how it would look. Does this look like it would be great on a coffee mug? Would it fit on a shirt? Could it display well on a web browser?

After refining your design a few times, send it out to a website that takes in such items. Choose a proper firm based on what you wish to make out of your artistic creation.

Chapter 6 – Create YouTube Videos

YouTube is one of the most exciting websites around. It has become the top place for online videos for how it offers a variety of things for people to watch. From self-help and instructional videos to historic or informative files, people can enjoy YouTube for a variety of fun things. There are many entertaining videos that cover movies, video games and much more as well.

But some of the more popular YouTube videos are from people who have made names for themselves on the site. It seems as though people these days are becoming famous on YouTube. They just post a bunch of videos of themselves doing stuff and the next thing you know they are all over the place.

It is obvious that you aren't necessarily going to make millions of dollars off of YouTube videos like what so many others do. But you can still create YouTube videos with the intention of making money.

This comes from the advertising revenue that you will get off of those videos. Original videos can include advertisements that appear at varying times. They might appear before a video starts playing or in the middle. In other cases ads come in the form of popups that appear at random.

A YouTube user who has ads on one's videos will earn money for each time those messages are viewed. This total adds up over time to an extensive amount.

You don't have to become a massive YouTube celebrity to make passive income off of the site. But it does help to look at a few points for getting YouTube to work to your advantage.

What Are Your Videos About?

Create videos that are entertaining or informative. Make ones that are worthwhile based on what you are interested in. It is clear that you must work on content that you actually have a vested interest in. You don't want to make videos if you have no idea what you are discussing or you have no interest in the subject matter.

But when think about your interests, you should see if they are ones that are worth sharing with others. You might have an interest in playing a certain small-level sport like ultimate Frisbee or curling, for instance. Creating videos about those is great for how you are not only highlighting what you like but are also bringing it out to people who might be interested in such activities. These include people who are familiar with them and those who want to learn a little something more about your interests.

Search for your interests on YouTube to see if other people are covering them already. Look at what their videos are about in particular. As you do this, come up with unique ideas that have not been covered by those videos. You could fill in the gaps that have been left by all those people on YouTube.

How Many Videos?

Be advised when trying to create YouTube videos that you will need plenty of them for your efforts to be successful. You must get dozens of them ready for your site to become a trustworthy and appealing place for people to visit.

Keep on posting videos on a regular basis just to become visible. Having one or two in a week is always a good idea.

It can take a while to get all those videos that you want added onto your site. But when done right, it becomes easier for you to make money off of your YouTube channel.

Can You Choose Your Sponsor?

One issue to consider about using YouTube for passive income is that you might not always have the option to stick with certain kinds of sponsors. It most cases you have to only work with one or two particular sponsors. These are based on who is spending the most money to get onto YouTube.

Over time, your YouTube channel will become a little more recognized. The keywords on your videos and the links that come into and out of those videos will pair up with particular advertisements. Such ads are more relevant to your needs and the desires of the people who want the videos.

When those ads become relevant, people are more likely to click on their links. They may also be more likely to actually watch those ads and not click the skip button to get straight to your video. Your potential for profits will increase when people actually interact with or watch those ads. But again, this only works when people watch your videos on a regular basis.

Exercise

Look at what you are interested in and create plans for videos based on that interest. Plan out some topics you want to discuss. Create individual videos for each of those topics or subjects to introduce.

Record videos that are carefully orchestrated. Establish a script for each video and check on the technical features of each video. Everything you prepare should be professional in its appearance. Don't upload stuff that looks like you just spent a few minutes throwing everything together.

As you create those videos, plan a schedule for when each of those videos will be introduced. Look at how you will post them based on their descriptions too.

When this works, your YouTube page becomes more interesting. It especially comes as people notice that you are a more reliable and trustworthy source for information on something.

Chapter 7 – Renting Out Items

The last of the options to look into for earning passive income involves taking assets that you already have and letting people use them. The process requires a bit of effort on your hand as it requires you to have particular assets on hand. But it could provide you with passive income as it works.

With this, you will allow other people to enjoy what you have and make money off of it. You don't even have to be around for people to take in your items.

You have probably been hearing about crowd sharing in recent time. With people looking for ways to save money on accommodations, vehicle rentals and such, they are turning to everyday people for help.

They know that rentals are cheaper when they contact people directly through crowd sharing websites. The variety of things available for rent is also greater. A car rental company can only offer so many types of vehicles.

With crowd sharing, a person could go online and find any car that could be rented out. The vehicle could be a basic passenger car for a long business trip. Maybe the car might be something fancy that could be rented out for a wedding. Whatever the case is, the selection that someone has should be greater when going online.

For instance, you could rent out your home to someone while you are out of town or you could allow someone to stay in a room for a period of time. You might also make a vehicle in your garage accessible to someone for a few hours at a time. Anything that is lying around in your home or is not used could provide you with passive income in the form of people renting out what you have.

A plan for renting out items works with a few steps. First, you will go to a site that allows you to list items that you want to rent out. Places like Airbnb have become very popular for this purpose.

You would have to list details on whatever it is you want to rent out to people. It might include something like a spare room in your home that is not used all that often. Maybe you have a vehicle that is not used regularly and could be offered to someone else for a bit.

As you rent these items out, you would charge people a certain amount of money for using them. That total would vary based on the particular items you are renting out and the money you agree to charge.

You will earn a particular total based on the charge that the site incorporates plus the fees that the hosting site that you list your item on charges. The totals can add up over time if you regularly let out something to other people.

A Word of Caution

As appealing as this option might be, you would have to watch for the terms associated with letting out items to other people. Make sure you only offer items that you know are safe to let other people use.

Watch for how you are maintaining whatever you have to provide to clients. You must keep your home, car or other property that you will make available in the best possible condition.

This is to not only ensure it is suitable for use but also to show clients that you care. It is often easier to make money this way if you show that you put in enough effort for letting products out in a responsible manner.

Also, look at how often you would plan on offering your items. You don't want to chase people off by needing to share things at a certain time that might be inconvenient for some.

Many places that let you rent things out give you the option to keep certain items off limits for specific periods of time. These include cases where you need to use something for yourself and you cannot get anyone else to use an item for a particular time.

Also, any contracts involved with the rental process should be understood and analyzed. Review what a website or other rental service provider will demand from you.

Exercise

Look at a space in your home or other large item that could be made available for someone. Do you use a certain room all that often? Is there a vehicle that just lies there in your garage? Perhaps you have some yard equipment that could be made available.

Figure out what is dormant in your space and find a site that lets you list items available for rent in your local area. Look at the available times you have for letting people use something. Keep whatever is listed properly maintained. Check all parts of whatever you are offering and clean off anything that you've got.

Take pictures to show that what you have is functional and appealing. Those pictures should go right on your online listing.

Think about some questions that people might ask about whatever you are offering. Look for answers relating to how certain items are to be offered and be prepared to address them.

As you come across the right plans, you will find that it is not too hard to get passive income over the things that you already have in your home. Take advantage of whatever is just sitting around and find ways to make them more visible and useful. The money you will get off of them will add up after a while.

Chapter 8 – Rental Property Investing

In the recent past, topics on investments in rental property have taken center stage in most discussions. The main reason is the belief by most people that investment in rental property is a business which is only reserved for the very rich. This myth further proceeds that without wealth it is almost impossible to own rental property.

The main purpose of this book is to try and demystify this myth by giving a step by step account of how one can go about the business of renting property. It delves deep into the major areas of the industry which most investors do not understand. It tries to help potential as well as existing investors on the best approach to operate and manage a rental property for a higher return on investment. Furthermore, it acts as a guide to investors on how best one can acquire financing to develop a rental property and how they can manage the property for maximum returns.

In view of the ever-changing environment in the rental property industry, the book attempts to inform the reader on the various means available that can be utilized to update oneself with the right perspective of the industry. It touches on the importance of working with a team of professionals in the industry to make the right decisions regarding the management of rental property.

This book also lays emphasis on the importance of self-education as a rental property investor to be well conversant with the industry including how it operates and the best way of managing the property. It provides guidance to the investor on how he can be able to set the right prices or rent for his property and how he can improve his cash flow and passive income. It goes into details on the best approach to use when renting your property and how you can prepare legal documents for your own protection.

At the end of it all, the book attempts to educate the reader on the best way to invest in rental property and the best way to manage it. The primary objective is that anybody can invest in rental property and get maximum returns on investments.

In simple terms investment property is an investment that is primarily purchased to generate income. This type of property is one that is bought for the purposes of either renting it out or reselling it for a profit after undertaking some renovations. There are, however, some variations of this term. One such variation is an instance where a family decides to downsize or relocate to another residence. This property can become an investment property if the family decides not to sell it. Another example is where one purchases a house that hosts many families. The new owner might decide to live in one of the houses and rent the others. There is also another variation where he owners of the property might decide to be using the property once in a while or during certain seasons as vacation destinations.

Certainly, having an investment property comes with several benefits. These benefits include:

Potential for double profits

An investment property has the ability to offer two possibilities for financial gain. These two possibilities include rent paid by the tenants to the owner of the property and the resultant appreciation in the value of the property when it is later resold. The rent can offer a good passive ongoing income to the property owner. There is also the possibility of benefitting from available tax advantages.

This makes investment properties to attract a large number of investors because they are known to have better returns on investments as opposed even to investments in the stock market. For instance, it is known that the stock market is very volatile and the risk of losing out on investments are very high. However, the rental property market is quite stable with high chances of rising prices.

Easy capitalization

It is possible to venture into the rental property market with little or no money for capitalization as opposed to trading on the stock market. One has various alternatives of financing which include loans that can be acquired without using so many financial resources. This, therefore, enables you to use your liquid cash assets for other investment opportunities.

FACTORS TO CONSIDER BEFORE INVESTING

There are several factors to consider before making a decision on investing in investment or rental property. Let us look at some of them.

Rental property versus budget

Investments in property are one of the most effective ways of creating wealth. It can also become a liability that can steal your precious time and drain away your hard-earned resources.

It is, therefore, prudent to have a solid financial plan which will reinforce your belief in your rental property business. It is advisable to engage professionals in the field by always consulting your accountants and real estate attorneys. These are people who will help your out to realize our goals. You should be able to know from them issues such as your liquidity, the status of your retirement savings, and if your investment property can afford you a decent passive income even if your cash flow becomes predictable. You should also be able to know if your rental property has the capacity of providing you with an immediate income or a long-term appreciation.

The landlord question

If your financial situation is sufficient to enable you to invest in rental property, it is important to consider whether you will be in a position of taking up the responsibilities of becoming a landlord. This is an extremely challenging position that needs dedication and commitment. The management of a rental property will demand a certain amount of time and effort. However, you also have the option of engaging professionals to manage your property. The decision to be a hands-on or hands-off landlord will be your prerogative. Nonetheless, whichever management style you choose to adopt you must always ensure that you are always well informed so as to perfectly understand how this business venture runs.

It is advisable to link up with local real estate and /or landlord groups that have regular meetings.

This will help you to gain insider information from professionals such as accountants, attorneys, repair specialists and many others.

You will be able to be up to date with matters related to landlords/tenants, rental/lease agreements, access to trade journals and magazines and many other matters that are related to the rental property industry.

The location factor

Investing in rental property will give you various options to pursue. You can acquire rental property almost anywhere. You can have a team of experts manage your property thousands of miles away as an absentee landlord.

However, a large number of landlords prefer having their rental property near them. This is because this option affords certain advantages. It is easier to make good investment decisions when one is familiar with his surroundings. It also enables one to have good purchasing opportunities and comparable values.

Typical rental property

Most people wonder whether there is a typical rental property that can offer an investor maximum returns on investment.

It should be noted that any kind of rental property has the potential of generating sufficient passive income to the landlord.

It does not matter if the rental property is a single-family house, a cottage, a high-rise building, apartment building or a condo, all these properties have the ability to sustain a handsome profit.

Rental property suitability

When investing in rental property it is important to consider what type of property you need to have.

Should you invest in a high-rise building or a small single family house?

The decision will depend on your budget and objectives. However, for first-time investors, it is advisable to invest in a small way. The reason is simply that it takes some time before one can get a stable income from his investment. During this period one is also obligated to do loan repayments which, in most cases, come from regular income. It is, therefore, good to invest in a small property which will translate into smaller repayment amount. The next thing to consider is where your rental property should be located. Should you locate your property in the city or the country side? Should it be a resort or a residential property? These are issues you have to consider to determine the suitability of your property.

SEARCHING FOR RENTAL PROPERTY

When shopping for a rental property it is always good to have a written pre-approval from a lender. This will act as a ticket to gain the attention of real estate sellers and agents. This is because the pre-approval acts as a guarantee or security that the financing will go through. It also has many other benefits which include:

- **Having the full knowledge of the amount of money that you can afford for the investment**
- **Having the advantage of getting the best bargain in the market**
- **Knowledge regarding the type of investment you are looking for**
- **Fast and simple loan processing after identifying your investment**

The main reason why you are buying the property to get a profit and generate ongoing income. This is something you should always consider so that you can seek for the best offer that will give you an added advantage. It is good to set your price range and target the most suitable areas for investing. You can do this by using Multiple Listing services by real estate agents or newspaper classified section.

It is good to choose active locations that have facilities for shopping, recreation, nightlife, culture and many others.

It is also good to consider about resale prospects and whether the property is in an area where it can attract tenants.

It is also good to focus on the purchase price and the rental income that it might generate. The property should also be in the proximity of schools and learning institutions. This is good for tenants with children and also raises the profile of your property.

It is recommended that you look for simple homes which is easy to maintain and which has appeal. In the case of renovations, it is good to do the work quickly and put it on the market as soon as possible. It is good to let experts do the marketing for you so that you can get a tenant as soon as possible. A good way to find a good property is searching for distressed properties which have been foreclosed and are in the hands of the lenders. You can find these in online foreclosure listings. You can also use the word of mouth in your search for a rental property by talking to potential property sellers and letting them know that you are in the market for the rental property. There is also a good possibility of getting a good bargain from out-of-state sellers by checking at the tax assessor's office.There are many other ways in which you can search for the right rental property.

Other methods include leaving pre-printed cards in people's mailboxes in a neighborhood that you are interested in. You can also do "wanted" ads on bulletin boards, local newspapers, groceries, stores and even community websites. With a well-developed plan, it won't take long before the search for your preferred rental property becomes a reality.

BUILD A TEAM OF EXPERTS

Acquiring rental property can be made easy if you work with a team of experts in your endeavors. The first experts to deal with include your attorney and tax advisor to advise you on the viability of making this purchase and also about the tax benefits that you may accrue.

Real estate agent

The other important expert you have to work with is the real estate agent. This agent is very useful especially if you have a rental property that is far off. Real estate agents will act as your representatives and keep you informed on the type of property you require. Here are some of the things that an estate agent can do for you.

- Will meet your property investment needs
- Provide important information on property related issues such as taxes, comparable values, building codes regulations, rental amounts etc.
- Help you to draft an offer on any property you wish to buy
- Acts as a go-between between you and the seller and helps in the negotiation process.

Appraiser

Another important expert you will deal with is an appraiser. This is a professional who is able to evaluate the value of your rental property and advise your investment is financially okay. Most lenders actually need properties to be appraised so that they know if the property has the right value that can necessitate funding.

Although you can find out the prices of such property from newspapers by price comparisons, it is good to hire an appraiser. The appraiser can help you determine the current market value of the property you intend to purchase. He is able to do a review of recently sold properties in the area and do a comparative analysis of the same using his technical expertise.

Investment property financing expert

You also need an investment property financing expert who is able to offer you important financing information. They are also able to help you with issues related to mortgages and their customization to suit your specific needs.

SELF-EDUCATION

The ability to rent your investment property will greatly determine your success. It is, therefore, imperative to ascertain that your investment has the potential to generate sufficient profit to justify its viability. Take the initiative to know all about landlord and tenant laws by consulting with your legal representatives on laws and ordinances in your jurisdiction which are applicable to your rental property.
A good example is the Federal Housing Act that prohibits

discrimination in rental, finance, and sale of residential property based on color, race, sex, religion, nationality, familial status, or disability.

You can also use the internet to download forms an information online or visit your local office that deals with landlord/tenants affairs or the attorney general's office. You should also try and find out if your jurisdiction provides regulations limiting the amount of chargeable rent.

There are also instances where neighborhood associations, zoning restrictions, or condo associations make it illegal for landlords to rent their property or subdivide it into units. You should, therefore, ensure that you're your investment objectives are within the purview of the law. On the issue of appreciation, it is important to consult with your local chamber of commerce or your real estate agent to know the number of homes in your neighborhood whose value has appreciated in the recent past. If the answer is I the affirmative, you will know that your investment choice is viable in the long run even if it is still struggling to break even.

Projecting Your Rent

To reasonably project how much rent you can charge for your rental property, start by visiting the website of authorities that regulate the industry such as the US Department of Housing and Urban Development. This website can give you information that breaks down the average rentals in your respective jurisdiction.

The statistics are usually based on the number of bedrooms in a property and this will enable you to adjust your rent either upwards or downwards. You can also use the local newspapers by going through the rent section. You will then be able to track rents for properties that are similar to yours for a given period of time. This information can also be provided by your real estate agent.

CASH FLOW CALCULATIONS

To determine how much your potential rental property is worth and how much profits it can generate for you as rent, you need to calculate its cash flow. The calculations involved are simple. All you need to do is to add up our regular costs which include insurance, mortgage repayments, marketing or advertisement investments, property tax, utility costs that the tenant is not required to pay, and a 5% emergency or backup fund. All these expenses should be subtracted from the rent so as to determine your monthly cash flow.

If you intend to purchase a rental property that is used for the same purpose it is important to ask the seller for the Schedule E documentations which can show any loss of income on the property. You should then consult your accountant to find out if such losses can be claimed from your income tax.

An overview may show that one can claim rental losses if his annual earnings are less than $100,000.

You can be limited to the deductibility of your rental losses if your annual income is $100,000. On the other hand, if our annual income is over $150,000 you are not liable to claim for any loss in rental income.

Rent Your Property

It is important to find good renters because they not only safeguard your property but also protect and take care of your property. They are profitable because they stay for a long time and reduce vacancy time and eliminate unnecessary expenses. Studies show that it costs more looking for a new tenant that keeping an old one. It is important to motivate good tenants in many ways including a small rent reduction or offering some gifts. The question is where one can find a good tenant. One can use the expertise of a rental agent who is able to find good tenants for a small fee. You can also market your rental property through word of mouth or by using the classified ads. You should be clear and specific in your ad to save you from much trouble later. If you do not want smokers or pets in your house it is important to make the point clear. It is also important to consult your legal representative before doing the ads.

The best way to go is by setting your own standards and list all the requirements of the tenant and check them against the landlord-tenant laws. You should be able to deal with tenants with a good income and who have steady and stable jobs.

You should also be able to project the length of time such tenants have had in their last residence.

It is pertinent to avoid frequent turnover which has the capacity to affect your profits significantly.

Lease preparation

It is important to consult with your legal representative so as to get the lease prepared which covers both your concerns and also is applicable to given laws. States and jurisdictions have different restrictions regarding security deposits, rent amounts, and tenant rejections due to poor credit ratings. The lease is an important document which will act as your success blueprint.

Lease purchase option

It is also useful to know that there are other options which include the lease purchase option to your property. This type of option has the ability to attract a number of tenants who are able to handle monthly mortgage payments but not a down payment on the property.

The process involves leasing the house to a tenant who pays a specific monthly rent. This amount which is payable within a specific period of time is known as an option consideration and is divided into two. The first part of the payment is about 5% of the property's value and is non-refundable while the second part is the monthly payments that can go up to $300 that is paid together with the rent.

These payments are geared towards the purchase of the property at the end of the term.

However, if the renter makes a decision of not buying the property the landlord gets to keep the money. This is a very effective way of selling your property and ensures that you get your selling price no matter how the market looks like. This makes the tenants take good care of the property because they regard it as their own. However, many people think that it is not an effective method since some renters give up halfway their payments. To know if this method is effective it is good to consult your financial advisor or a local landlord association.

MAINTAIN YOUR RENTAL PROPERTY

The law requires you as the landlord to maintain your rental property to standards that are livable. Among the various requirements include having a property that has windows and doors with locks, a roof which is leak proof, a heating system that works. Different states have different requirements with respect to maintenance and repair responsibilities.

It is also your responsibility to keep your property in a good state to maintain its value.

You should, therefore, engage dependable repair people who will be able to prepare your property for your initial renters, meet tenant needs and also put the property in order for new tenants if your old tenants move out.

It is therefore important not to allow your property to stay vacant because you will be losing money in the process. In case you have purchased a co-op or condo, maintenance is usually paid for by your association fees.

In case your home is a bit far from your place of residence it will be hard for you to do some maintenance activities like repairing leaking faucets, snow removal or gutter cleaning. In this case, you need to make arrangements with a dependable handyman or engage the services of a maintenance company. Your real estate agent is able to recommend a good company for you. You can also use a home warranty service. This service charges an annual fee that covers the repair of all of your major appliances for a whole year.

If you are an absentee landlord, you can engage the services of a property manager. The manager will be charged with the responsibility of running your property, scouting for good repair people, does your book keeping and other important roles. He is also able to collect monthly rent on your behalf and can even organize for leases to your rental property. The property manager is able to relieve you of these duties but they have to be paid.

Most of them will usually go home with between 5%-10% of your gross income or more if additional services are provided. This is, however, a good bargain when you consider the amount of stress they would have relieved for you.

But you should always consider the costs involved, your tolerance level and work schedule before you make any decision.

If you engage the property manager it is important to break down all his duties and responsibilities in the contract.

LOAN APPLICATION

The rental property business is dependent on financing and it is important to include your lender as part of your team. Home mortgage consultants are specifically trained to interview finance seekers in a way that makes them understand his/her goals clearly. This helps them to make recommendations that help the finance seekers to develop their wealth potential in the business. These are professionals who can make you analyze your options and customize solutions to meet your particular needs.

There are a number of ways in which you can fund your investments and it is good to know your options depending on your budget, financial goals and needs. It is therefore advisable to go through these options with your lender so that you can be able to select the most suitable option at your disposal. There are a number of options that your lender can help you to ponder over.

Home equity financing

This type of financing takes advantage of the equity that you have for your primary residence to purchase a rental property. It is possible to borrow an amount that is equal to the value of your residence. However, this type of financing may be tax deductible.

Renovation financing

This type of financing is a one-time loan that equals the purchase price of a property that needs some renovation less the cost of renovating it. The amount is based on the higher value of the house after the said renovations have been done. This, therefore, gives you the privilege of enjoying the dividends of your rental property immediately.

Low down payment/ No down payment

These are options that make a home to become affordable right away. This type of financing allows one to pay for a property with out of pocket cash for you to be able to begin to profit from your investment right way.

No documentation/limited documentation option

This type of option is a smart choice for people who are self-employed whose incomes are not stable and keep on fluctuating from year to year. It is also suitable for people whose incomes are hard to document.

This flexibility excludes the finance seeker from the paper chase and makes his entry into property investment much easier.

Loan Closing Preparation

This is a four step loan closing procedure which will give you a general overview of what loan closing entails. The steps are as follows.

Appraisal

In this stage, your lender finds a professional appraiser whose duty is to determine the value of the rental property you want to purchase. The appraiser will give an estimate of the property by comparing it to others that have been recently sold in the locality. Lenders require the appraisal so as to ensure that the property that secures the loan will cover it in the case of any default.

Home inspection

It is advisable that any home buyer should be able to do a home inspection. In most cases, a home inspection is a requirement for in the home financing approval process. The inspection should cover all major areas of the home including electrical systems, foundation, heating and cooling systems, plumbing, roofing, and other exterior features.

Title insurance

Title insurance is of two types. One is for the protection of the lender and the other one protects the borrower from ownership claims on your property. These are claims which can be made by heirs of former owners, undisclosed spouses, creditors of former owners, or any other parties.

The lender will require you to buy the title property so that they can protect their interest in the transaction.

On the other hand, it is squarely your responsibility to buy the other title insurance to protect your interest in the property.

It is advisable to consult a mortgage advisor who will be able to recommend you to a title insurance company which will give you more information regarding this type of insurance.

Homeowners insurance

Home owner insurance is a necessary document that will be requested by the mortgage lender. This type of insurance covers losses such as fire. Burglary, tornadoes, and any other losses. It pays for damages that may happen as a result of these events. It also covers the costs of repair and replacement of lost contents. In case the property is damaged and becomes uninhabitable, the insurance is able to cover for additional living expenses for a certain period until the repair is fully undertaken. It also takes care of losses that result in injuries or their properties are damaged when they were on your property.

Closing

This is the stage that you go through all the final steps in getting the loan. It is important to note that all costs for closing should be fully paid. You will get to know how much you need to pay for closing from your mortgage consultant and attorney. This is important so as you can avoid unnecessary delays.

Conclusion

All of these ideas for getting the most out of your passive income plans are worth exploring. The chances that you have for getting money without putting in much effort over time will be worthwhile.

You must look into how well your plans for making passive income work though. Be certain you take a look at what you will be setting up in your process. Be aware of how you might have to spend some money to get a few of these plans running depending on what you might be working with.

Maintaining your passive income efforts is also important to consider. You must look at how well the income streams you take in are operated so they will be easy to follow.

Don't forget to think about how you will tackle some of these endeavors. Being creative and thoughtful in your plans will go a long way. It only takes a few bits of time at the start to give you a lifelong stream of income that can add up.

Good luck with your efforts in getting the most out of your passive income plans.

About Property Investing to sum it all, it is good for any new investor in rental property to get his/her facts right before venturing into the business that is hugely regarded as a business for the rich. Any investor - rich or not so rich, can invest in rental property by following the right procedure necessary to make it in the industry.

Before engaging in the business, you need to inform yourself on what the rental business entails. You should seek information about the business by talking to professionals in the field such as real estate agents, landlord associations, attorneys, financial advisors and many other professionals. They are able to offer you expert advice on the intricacies of the investment. You can also do your own research by educating yourself through trade magazines, journals and other documents that cover different areas related to investing in rental property. More information can also be found on different websites dealing with the same subject matter.

After gathering sufficient knowledge on the business, it is advisable to consider several factors before you make a decision of investing in the business.

Among the various factors to consider should include the value of the rental property you intend to invest in and whether your budget is sufficient to afford such an investment.

Other things to consider include the location of the property, the type of property you should invest in, and whether you will be able to take the responsibilities of being a landlord.

You should then begin the process of searching for the right rental property.

You can do this through a number of ways including placement of ads in local newspapers, consulting with real estate agents, searching for distressed rental property that have defaulted, etc. You also need a team of experts who will offer you advice on different areas of the business. These experts include real estate agents, appraisers, legal representatives, and even financial consultants.

After acquiring the most suitable rental property, you should immediately find the right tenant for renting.

 The tenant should be an individual who is financially stable and one who will not present problems in future. You should also set out your own rules and regulations which should be adhered to by the renter.

Maintenance of the property is also important. You should engage the services of handymen and repair people to maintain your house to the required standards.

You can also engage a property manager who can maintain the property on your behalf. By following this procedure you are sure of maintaining the value of your property and at the same time generate a reasonable income from it.

Your Gift!

We want to show our appreciation that you support our work, so we have put together a gift for you.

bit.ly/2xXbHO5

Just visit the link above to download it now.

We know you will love this gift. Thanks!

www.ingramcontent.com/pod-product-compliance
Lightning Source LLC
Chambersburg PA
CBHW050243230526
45470CB00005B/2089